*This book is dedicated to those who have supported me, inspired me and believed in me. You know who you are.*

# EDUCATION EXPOSED

Leading a school in a time of uncertainty

---

## SAMUEL STRICKLAND

**First Published 2020**

by John Catt Educational Ltd,
15 Riduna Park, Station Road,
Melton, Woodbridge IP12 1QT

Tel: +44 (0) 1394 389850
Email: enquiries@johncatt.com
Website: www.johncatt.com

**© 2020 Samuel Strickland**

**All rights reserved.**

No part of this publication may be reproduced, stored
in a retrieval system, transmitted in any form or by
any means, electronic, mechanical, photocopying,
recording, or otherwise, without the prior permission
of the publishers.

Opinions expressed in this publication are those
of the contributors and are not necessarily those
of the publishers or the editors. We cannot accept
responsibility for any errors or omissions.

**ISBN: 978 1 912906 29 1**

Set and designed by John Catt Educational Limited

# Contents

# Introduction:
# 'Shifting sands: Education, education, education'

This book is designed to serve as a dip in and dip out guide to a wide array of varying aspects of whole-school life, though it can be read in one full sitting. Each chapter is self-contained, providing a short and sharp insight into a specific aspect of school improvement.

When I commenced my life as an educator I was trained by Christine Counsell at the University of Cambridge. My PGCE in Secondary History was academically rigorous to say the least. The course consisted of an assertively strong approach to reading, reading, reading. Knowledge itself truly was power. This is a mantra that has stuck with me throughout my career. Christine was championing exactly the things then that she champions now. Namely, the curriculum serves as a progression model, the importance of in-depth and expert subject knowledge, a strong approach to routines for learning, a belief in subject communities and a moral purpose driven by a desire for social justice. None of this grounding has left me. However, my resolve and belief in these fundamentals has been challenged, at times waned and come under pressure by what I can only describe as a fad-driven approach to education that has engulfed our profession for a good 15 plus years.

As I moved into the world of being an NQT workload was not something that anyone discussed with any sense of intent nor was there really a view that something should be done to support staff with their workload. The motto 'sink or swim' really was held true and asking an eager and energised NQT to teach eight different subjects, five to A2 standard, was a challenge and a half. What shocked me more than anything during my formative years as a teacher was the speed of change, most of which was nonsensical. I worked in a fantastic school but there was always a sense that change, change and a little more change was both good and necessary to keep ahead of the game. I got it. I understood it. However, I didn't necessarily agree with it all.

As I moved into the lower echelons of middle management, as a Head of History, Lead Practitioner for Teaching and Learning and as a lead for SCITT, I was at times utterly shocked by what I witnessed. A time of 10-20% teacher talk crept in. Edutainment became the expected norm. Differentiation by task plagued us all. Everything was about pace, pace and a little more pace. If your lessons were not entertaining, not fast paced and not resource-rich then one would not be deemed an 'Outstanding' teacher, whatever that actually meant. Group work was rife. Think, pair, share, VAK, learning style questionnaires and so on, all flooded the INSET training airwaves. A five day AFL course run by the Local Authority at the time drilled into us all a belief that pupils retained 80-90% of what they taught one another and that differentiated learning objectives were the future. Bloom's Taxonomy was seen as the vehicle to judge lessons by. The list of edutainment approaches goes on and on. Inside the Black Box had been misinterpreted in the extreme.

As time moved on I hoped, prayed and wanted things to settle. I became sick of the expected voyages of discovery, international café lessons and endless card sorts for the sake of them. Sadly we then saw the rise and fall of assessment with, and then without, levels. Data hinged around flightpaths, with pupils expected to move in formulaic and robotic upward trajectories from one term or data capture to the next. They were expected to do this at light speed too, otherwise *you*, the teacher, had failed. Pupil Premium financial pump priming then came in. Yet it has done little in real terms to address the needs of these pupils as schools have used this money to pay for initiatives that add next to no value. A rise of gaming the system, with qualifications that can be achieved in a week and flood bucket three of your Progress 8 dominated school thinking. However, this set of approaches lacked any real thought bar getting Ofsted off our backs. Key Stage 3 became the wasted years as leadership teams wanted an elongated Key Stage 4 experience that allowed for results, results and more results. Results at what cost though?

We have also seen the rise of companies selling us magic silver bullets, with promises of seeing rapid and sustained progress if you follow formula X. Almost all of it has been tosh. Almost all of it has been at the expense of the very reason we have trained teachers to teach. They have been trained to be the experts *not* the guide from the side or the facilitator of games that somehow magically brings about learning. We have also been led to believe that learning can be measured. More so in a 15-minute snapshot, where pupils are measured against a skill-driven, differentiated learning objective. This has all been at the expense and loss of so many skilled teachers, skilled professionals, who became tired, jaundiced or simply flogged to death by extreme demands.

My career thus far has spanned an array of settings, from an Upper School, to an all girls' school, to a flagship school within a Trust, a free school and an extremely large all-though school. I have held numerous positions, most notably as a Director of Sixth Form for nearly five years and then as a Vice Principal for five and a half years. During my time as a Vice Principal I was in charge of student care, safeguarding, curriculum, the SEF, the SIP, Teaching and Learning, operated as a safeguarding lead and served as a primary governor. I also worked as an Associate Principal for a year. During my tenure as an Associate Principal, my school achieved GCSE and A Level results that received commendation from the DFE, Nick Gibb and the SSAT. I have also had the privilege to write and deliver national NPQ qualifications.

What I aim to do with this book is challenge some of the suggested norms that we are expected to accept as a profession and consider how things can potentially be otherwise done. Will everyone agree with me and my views? Absolutely not. Nor should they. I adore the fabric of discourse that fills our profession and see discussion, challenge and critique as a positive. I hope you find this book useful if nothing else.

The book is divided into five sections, with each section taking a major driver for school improvement. Section 1 focuses on leadership, Section 2 on behaviour, Section 3 on the curriculum, Section 4 on teaching and Section 5 on workload and professional development. As you read this book I would like you to consider carefully what you consider the inter-relationship between the Mother Ship (i.e. the school in its entirety) to be with all of the satellites that protrude from it (i.e. all of the subject domains within the school). This is key to how you run a school and the very decisions that you make.

# Section 1:

## Leading from the front, centre and rear

# Chapter 1:
# Leading, leading, leading

## Leadership is the capacity to translate vision into reality

### Common misconceptions

1. You have to change your leadership style on a regular basis, according to a situation.

2. You should operate as an island.

3. Being busy as a leader makes you visibly effective and making lots of regular changes is a positive and what people want.

What type of leader are you? Are you strategic? Are you someone who strives for excellence? Are you an operational manager? There is a lot to think about when you consider being a leader.

Being a leader is tough, it can be lonely, you can feel like an island operating in isolation. Sometimes, as a leader, you have to keep your powder dry, you have to keep your doubts to yourself and you have to abate negativity. Equally leading can be highly rewarding, exciting and you can feel very much like you are creating a team. Just remember, Rome was not built in a day!

Over the last few decades a lot has been made of leadership styles. Are you authoritarian, dictatorial, dogged, a devolved leader, compassionate, humble and so on. A lot has been made of how we respond to different situations. For example, do you decide on the basis of logic, using an analytical and impersonal approach or do you allow your values to dictate how you respond, using a more subjective and people-orientated approach? Are you the sort of person who likes to have everything meticulously planned or are you the type who allows nature to take its course and respond to events accordingly? I appreciate that these examples may seem binary.

The list of traits and characteristics that make a strong leader is almost endless. I have seen people peddle the idea that you should adopt and adapt a particular leadership style for any one given particular situation. This can, I would argue, cause confusion regarding the type of leader that you are. John Dunford once said, 'good leaders do not have a single leadership style. You adapt to suit the situation. The appropriate leadership style to develop a new school policy on teaching and learning is very different from the style adopted when the fire alarm goes off.'[1]

With Dunford's comments in mind, what leadership style would you adopt to these two differing scenarios:

> 1: One of your senior team line manages a BTEC subject and has unearthed a situation where the head of department has completely misunderstood the requirements of the Key Stage 4 specification. As a result, an entire year group has completed a raft of coursework that is irrelevant and 15 weeks of curriculum time has been lost. What do you do?

> 2: Ofsted last visited your school two years ago and you are not expecting them to come to your school for another year. However, you have just received a call from a lead HMI stating that your school will be going through a full inspection tomorrow. What do you do?

Whilst there is much to be appreciated with Dunford's stance I do feel adopting a different leadership persona or cloak is something to be

---

1. Dunford, J. (2011) 'Ten things learned on my leadership journey', John Dunford Consulting [Online] November 1. Retrieved from: www.bit.ly/2Z0FhjB

wary of. By changing your leadership style you will be changing your demeanour, manner and how you come across to others. Ultimately you need to be true to yourself, your personality, your strengths and areas to develop. Leadership style surveys are probably as useful as learning style surveys.

A key starting point for anyone considering moving into leadership is that you must at first understand yourself fully before you can lead anyone else. You must know what you stand for, what defines you, what your moral compass is, how you think, how you act, how you treat others and how you deal with stress, problems and crises. I have personally found Boyatzis' model of 'the ideal self' really useful here as a starting point.[2] First you need to carefully consider who you are at this current moment in time, then consider your strengths and then consider what you would like your ideal self, as a leader, to be. Very simply this can be mapped out as follows:

A lot has been made of what makes a successful leader. If you look at any leadership orientated job advert you will see an array of superlatives, mostly focusing on being a superhero or superhuman. The reality is the traits expressed in most job adverts are a work of fiction. The very best leaders are authentic, humble, flexible, willing to learn from others, often experienced or show a propensity to learn very quickly. Most of all, the very best leaders are human and never forget what it is like to be one of the troops. The very best leaders have a deep understanding of themselves, in terms of their values, beliefs, moral purpose and vision.

---

2. Boyatzis, R. (2002) 'Unleashing the Power of Self-Directed Learning', in R. R. Sims (ed) *Changing the Way We Manage Change*. Santa Barbara, CA: Greenwood Publishing Group.

A useful model to analyse yourself against is the Johari Window Model but, as with any self-assessment tool, you have to be fully honest with yourself. The window is divided into four sections. Firstly there is the open or free area, which outlines what information you know and what you want others to know. For example, you may share details about you, your vision, your approach here. Then we have the blind area. This area details what you do not know about yourself but what others know about you. This is where feedback from others comes into play. The third area is the hidden area. This is what you know about yourself that others do not. Often sensitive information about yourself will reside in this area. The final area is the unknown area. This is what is unknown to both yourself and others. For example, feelings, behaviours or attitudes. The window looks as follows:

|  | Known to self | Not known to self |
|---|---|---|
| Known to others | Shared | Blind |
| Not known to others | Hidden | Unknown |

As a tool the Johari Window Model can be useful to get you to think carefully about yourself but it can also be useful to ask others, close to you and who know you well, to create a window for you. As with any self-evaluation confidentiality, trust and respectful honesty are key.

It is really important to define your values, what is important to you and what your beliefs are. How you deal with key situations, both in terms of the decisions you make and how you make them, will define you, your tenure and how you are perceived. Moral dilemmas can test us to the full. For example, how would you deal with this situation:

'You have been given an allocation for Pupil Premium funding and your school has directed you to spend this money on additional one-to-one tuition to ensure that there are no gaps in your GCSE results data at the end of the year. Your school policy says it must be spent only on those children who are eligible. However, in the Year 11 cohort that you are working with, six children who are eligible for the funding are actually high attaining pupils on entry who are academically performing significantly ahead of their peers. There are six other children who are not eligible for this funding but would benefit from some direct intervention, utilising the Pupil Premium funding. These pupils are significantly behind their peers and unlikely to achieve a grade 4 in maths and English. What will you do? It is situations like this that can really test our moral purpose, our values and our beliefs. You need to be mentally prepared for situations like this.'

You need to accept that people will judge you. From the very first moment someone meets you, you will be judged. People will form a view as to the type of leader you are. It is really important that you stay true to yourself and do not allow anyone else to define who you are. It is really easy to allow someone's first impression of you to form a narrative about you. To allow this to cause you to fall into a mould that someone else is trying to craft. Do not let that happen. Be your own person. Be you. Equally, make sure that you have a plan for how you want to lead and run your department, area of the school or school itself. This will be discussed in more detail in chapter two. Always keep firmly at the forefront of your mind what your moral purpose is and, if you believe you are acting for the greater good or doing the right thing, do not be derailed by others.

Where you do encounter negativity, and you certainly will, do not allow this to define you. Do not allow negativity to take over. If you allow negativity to take hold of you it will consume and paralyse you. It will cause you to make irrational decisions, potentially rushed decisions. You are far better placed turning negatives into positives and always be solution focused. When something does go wrong learn from it. Think long and hard about why situation X did not go in your favour and consider carefully what the key take homes are.

It is important as a leader to be highly reflective. Every single day you will make hundreds of mini-decisions. It is really important that you compartmentalise these but equally important that you take time to reflect, for a few minutes a day at most, on what you did, why you did it and how you can be better tomorrow. If you do make mistakes, which you will, do not allow the mistakes to win, to take over and to consume you. If you make a mistake then acknowledge it, accept it and move on. You cannot change it and beating yourself up over it will do you little to no good. The issue with a mistake is that you are your own worst self-critic. The war with the mistake really is between you, the mistake and your brain. Most people won't care or will be too busy and preoccupied to notice your *faux pas*.

Ensure you are humble with your approach to leading but this humility has to be both authentic and felt. If you are putting on a sense of humility as a front then you are, by very virtue of your approach, being disingenuous. Avoid being the person who wants to always be right, whether that be because you are too proud to admit you may be wrong or because you see it as a sign of weakness. Adapting to new information, new ideas or a constructive critique is a sign of strength. It shows that you are reflective, attentive, capable of listening. If you stick resolutely to *your* plan you may well find that you lose the respect of your staff or your team. This is the beginning of the end. That said, watch out for what I call the 'know-it-alls.' In reality they know very little and are often full of bravado, suffering from the Dunning Kruger effect. We have all encountered people who are convinced that they know everything and want to convince you that they know everything. Be cautious of these people. These people will become a drain on you.

When you build your team do not surround yourself with carbon copies of yourself. Try and create a team around you that is different, varied and approaches situations in a differing way. If you create a team of clones your school will never truly advance. Whilst consistency is crucial to creating certainty within a school, you do need a team of people surrounding you who are capable of questioning you, positively of course. You also need to spread your net wide and create a network of people you can call upon for help, support, advice and guidance. You can never have enough sounding boards. I would always be wary of writing people off as well. Sometimes we can be hasty in our judgements and views of people and sometimes in our haste we make the wrong call.

The very best leaders instil belief in their team. You want your team to believe that they are the best. As a leader you need to allow this to perpetuate, to become a shared mindset, even if it is a myth. What is crucial and key, though, is that you do not become arrogant and complacent with it. The most skilled leaders will recognise when their team is surfing, swimming or sinking.

Taking your time is also key. Do not rush decisions. Equally, do not be frightened of making a decision. Temptation is your biggest Achilles here. When things are going badly, when you are faced with a difficult, testing or consuming situation, there is always a temptation to go for the quick and easy win. Often this is not the smartest or best play. Often this will cause longer term issues and often the tempting play has unintended consequences that you probably had not considered.

Sitting tight and waiting intelligently can be one of the hardest things to do but this is such a key trait of the best leaders. Taking your time over a decision, action or approach is hard. It is unpredictable though and hugely powerful. People often expect fast decisions, fast actions, for there to be a high speed impact. Human nature is to be busy, to work at speed. Surely if we work at steam, fire out lots of emails and key actions then we have done our job? I would argue that this is wrong, flawed and a sign of a weak or misguided leader. The first obstacle to overcome when you take your time over a decision is yourself. You must fight the inner mental voice that says you are being lazy. Worse still, a narrative forms that you are being weak or waiting because you cannot make a decision. Repel these thoughts when they form. If you are adopting an approach of intelligent waiting then have a plan, communicate this plan systematically and effectively, train people in how your plan works and their role within it. The key is to have the strength of character to sit tight and believe in your plan and your approach. Ensure that you hit your key milestones when you intended and stay tactical in your approach.

## Final thoughts

As chapter one draws to a close, keep in mind that measured, strategic, thoughtful and authentic leadership is a major school improvement driver. The key take away points from this chapter are:

1. Stay true to yourself and be your own person.

2. Do not allow negativity, fear, the worry of failure and the views of others to suffocate you.

3. Do not allow mistakes to consume you.

4. Build a team, not carbon copies of yourself.

5. Taking your time over decisions can be extremely powerful.

# Chapter 2:
# The vision for leading

## 'Preparation is key: If you want peace, prepare for war.'

### Common misconceptions

1. You need to make fast, high speed changes to be successful.

2. What worked in your previous context is transferable to all other contexts.

3. Taking your time over decisions is a weakness and a sign of indecision.

Prior planning prevents poor performance. My dad told me this repeatedly as a child and, my word, is he right. During the lame duck period, before you take over a school and are diligently seeing out your old role, you need to use this time to plan and prepare for your new role. You need to ready yourself for what is coming as much as you can because nothing truly prepares you for the hot seat.

Hearing the words 'you got the job' is beyond euphoric and after the climax of heightened positive emotions and feeling on top of the world, the mental reality sinks in that you have indeed got the job. Invariably people will ask you what you intend to do, to change, to sort, to drive and to make your own when you become a middle leader, senior leader or head. My view is that you should start by doing nothing, absolutely nothing! The strongest piece of advice I can give to anybody is to take your time.

Everything and anything is seductive and the rule book is there to lure you in. High speed wins; game, game some more and game a little more. Showing people who is boss, flexing your professional muscles and asserting yourself may seem like the right thing to do but I would argue they are not. A key to starting off life in a new school, irrespective of what position or role you will perform, is to get to know your setting, context and the people within it. Every school has its own culture, its own approach, its own 'way' and going in like a bulldozer can, in many cases, lead to your falling flat on your face.

In anticipation of becoming a principal in a new school I would advocate the following stages of preparation:

## Stage 1: Plan

I would highly recommend that you read, read and read some more. Immerse yourself in the latest thinking, in the long-standing theories, in the differing ends of the educational spectrum. Galvanise and assimilate as much information as you can. If you have the luxury of time, visit a number of schools and gather ideas. While doing this think really carefully about how you are going to present yourself as the head, what your identity will be and how you want to be perceived. Take time to consider what you want your senior team to look like, what your vision and values actually are and how this will manifest itself into your school's culture. Think also about how you want to be known by the staff, pupils, parents, governing body and the local community.

While reading take the time to plan every single area of your school out, even if sketchily. Consider how your ideal curriculum would and should look, what quality assurance should look like, how each subject area should look, your approach to student care, behaviour, workload and so on.

The key thing when you start in your new school is that no one will know who you are but everyone will expect you to have a view, opinion or stance, irrespective of what aspect of school life it may be. Having the comfort blanket of a well prepared whole-school plan, with the devil in the detail for each key area, will serve you well.

## Stage 2: Visiting before you start

I cannot emphasise or recommend enough the need to visit your new school several times before you start for real. Remember though, despite having not actually started as 'the boss' everyone will see you as 'the boss.' Think carefully about what you wear, how you present yourself and what you say. As much as you are going into your new school to ascertain the lie of the land you need to keep firmly in mind that the staff will be evaluating and pre-judging you. First impressions really do count.

During this stage I would personally seek to meet your senior team on a one-to-one basis. Get to know who they are, what their role is, how they view their role and the school, get to know them as a person. This is extremely important and an invaluable use of your and their time. If you get this wrong the damage will take a long time to repair. If you get it right you can very quickly build a team and a group of advocates. Your inner cabinet will make or break you as a principal, especially a new one. Likewise, get to know your PA (if you have one). The role of the PA is incredibly important and this person will serve as a real bedrock for you; assuming you have the right balanced professional relationship with them.

I would also seek to attend a governing body meeting in this pre-joining stage and, if possible, go for a meal with the chair and the deputy chair. Your bond with the chair really is critical.

During this phase you really are fact finding and creating an impression. I recommend going back to your ideal school vision in Stage 1 again and taking a little more time to consider and reconsider how you want your school to look.

## Stage 3: The first day

This is it! The *big day*! You have your best outfit on, a new pair of shoes and you look the part. Inevitably you are in school early but the realisation sinks in 'I am now the **boss**! I am in charge!' Day 1 really is key; this is genuinely make or break. Do not sit in your office. Do not spend the day sorting out your desktop, putting the good luck plant you have been given on a table. Make yourself a very visible presence. Walk the school, walk it a lot. Get your bearings. Speak to staff, parents and students. Make a nuisance of yourself. If there is only one thing that you do on day 1, ensure that you address the staff in a formal setting, Make the staff aware of who you are, what you expect, your moral compass and where you see the school heading. This is, in essence, your vision in a nutshell. Engage the staff in a quick SWOT analysis of the school. Within eight minutes you could be awash with incredibly powerful and honest feedback about your new school. Take that feedback home that night and marry it up against your thought processes in Stage 1. It may be that some of your thoughts prior to joining the school now need reconsidering.

## Stage 4: Communication

This is where 'I am going to do nothing' really comes in. This is highly powerful. Taking your time is highly powerful. Demonstrating patience and an ability to wait, listen, digest and then make changes is highly powerful. During Stage 4, I recommend that you do the following:

- Take every single assembly.
- Front up all staff briefings and staff meetings.
- Walk the corridors of the school, lots.
- Meet every single member of staff; be it one on one, in group forums or via an invite to meet the principal for tea and cake.
- Meet groups of pupils from every year group.
- Meet parents, especially at parent consultation evenings.
- Meet all of the governors.

- Repeat your messages, vision and values over and over. Do not underestimate the power of over-communication.

- Establish a clear meeting schedule for your senior team to meet with you one on one and as a team in its entirety. Your leadership and management of your senior team is critical.

- Begin to break down all of the aspects of the school and marry them up against your thought processes in stage 1.

- Ensure your school's safeguarding processes are exactly how they should be. If not, change them straight away. If these are an issue you may find your tenure in charge is a short-lived one.

## Final thoughts

To bring chapter two to a close, here are the key take away points that you need to consider:

1. Plan carefully how you want your school to look and feel.

2. Take your time to meet every member of staff and take a real interest in everyone.

3. Be highly visible, so everyone gets to know who you are, what you stand for and that you are a presence.

# Section 2:

## Behaviour, behaviour, behaviour

# Chapter 3:
# Behaviour, behaviour, behaviour

## 'Behaviour unlocks everything'

### Common misconceptions

1. Poor behaviour is the teacher's fault.

2. Good planning leads to good behaviour.

3. Routines and rules stifle creativity.

4. Behaviour management should respond and react to negative behaviours once they arrive.

5. Telling people what your policies and expectations are is enough.

'They behave for me mate' are five of the deadliest words to ever echo the staffroom. You have just had the lesson from hell. It is period 5 on a wet and windy Friday and colleague X utters this killer phrase to you. Nothing makes a teacher feel more insignificant and useless than hearing this utterly useless statement of bravado. When this statement is banded across the staffroom you know that teacher natural selection is being promoted by a school. It truly is a case of survival of the fittest.

Ultimately, poor behaviour is kryptonite to a school's culture. It is key that we get behaviour right. It will define the culture of a school. Positive behaviour will also reverse the Matthew Effect and support with social justice, for the most disadvantaged are potentially subjected to the lowest of behavioural expectations in our schools. If this is reversed then their true potential is unlocked. Positive behaviour allows all pupils ultimately to achieve as time, energy and effort is not being wasted on dealing with behaviour management. Instead it can be devoted to curricular design, upskilling subject knowledge and curriculum enactment.

Positive behaviour is also the strongest form of marketing for a school. Parents ultimately want it. Pupils want it. Staff need it. It will also assist with both your recruitment and retention of staff and pupils alike. If you truly want to support staff, support their workload, support their well-being, support their mental health and support their desire to work for you then deal with and resolve behaviour as an institutional issue. Behaviour should be taught. It is a subject in its own right and every bit as important as maths, English and science. Controversially, no doubt, I would argue that teaching behaviour is the number one priority for any school. Over and above all other school improvement priorities, strategies and approaches this is the one that yields the greatest impact, that makes or breaks a school, that allow teachers to teach and that gets results.

A key point that I want to emphasise is that we permit what we promote and we promote what we permit. With that in mind we should challenge some popular misconceptions around behaviour. Namely, good planning results in good behaviour. This has been banded around for many years and even cited in national professional qualifications. I challenge this stance. I could have the most meticulously planned lesson but if the climate for learning is poor in my school then the chances are my lesson will fall flat on its face. Equally another common myth is that poor behaviour is the teacher's fault. This again should be challenged and is often lazy gaslighting on the part of senior staff seeking to absolve their responsibility for behaviour. Another key myth that needs challenging is the notion that routines, structures and systems are somehow bad. They somehow stifle freedom and creativity. At best, this is a weak narrative.

There does need to be an awareness and an acceptance that dealing with behaviour is not easy. Dealing with and changing behaviour will take time. It requires effort, determination and relentless follow through. We also need to keep firmly in our minds that the vast majority of teachers can actually teach and that poor behaviour is kryptonite to their ability to enact the curriculum in the manner that they would like to. We should also avoid looking out for silver bullets or the latest set of fads and gimmicks.

A huge issue with behaviour is just how little training, as a profession, we receive. At most behaviour was an after-thought on my PGCE course. I remember having a one hour workshop on utilising the range of my voice, raising my eyebrows and holding my hands out with my palms facing down. Following this hour I was now 'behaviour ready.' Sadly little has changed throughout my career, be it via school INSET or national professional qualifications. Behaviour management is simply either not taught or, if it is, it is done very badly. Most behaviour management consequently ends up being reactive. This is compounded by the fact that over a fifth of teachers think that behaviour is not good in our schools.

One of the biggest myths banded around in schools is that behaviour, poor behaviour, is the teacher's fault. If the pupils have misbehaved then it is somehow the teacher's fault for not having planned a lesson that is entertaining, highly paced, challenging and engaging. Convenient and weakly devised narratives such as 'you need to go faster', 'you need to be more engaging', 'you need to differentiate more', have surfaced. These narratives place behaviour firmly at the door of the teacher and make any issues with behaviour their fault. I do accept that a superbly enacted lesson can assist with pupil behaviour but I do not believe that an incredibly well planned lesson, endless streams of worksheets and card sorts will lead to amazing behaviour. I could have organised for Ronaldo, Messi or the Pope to address my class or a year group but if the school culture and climate for learning is poor, weak or flawed then there will be poor behaviour. The narrative that teachers are to blame is one that needs quashing.

There has been a lot discussed and even written in the last year and a bit about culture, character and the need for a member of the senior team to be responsible for driving this. The view being that this will somehow promote positive behaviour and flip a school's culture positively on its head. Whilst I understand the logic and reasoning behind this ideal, I do think it is missing a trick. The behaviour within a school, which encompasses its culture, climate and ethos, all come first and foremost from the will of one person, the principal/head. Of course the senior team, middle leaders and every other stakeholder have to buy into that vision and support in driving it. If this did not happen then a principal would face a *coup d'etat* and probably find that their tenure in office is short lived. However, whatever the person at the top defines as the school's vision, whatever they permit and whatever they promote, will become the school culture, will set the behaviour barometer. It is, in most cases, foolhardy to think otherwise. A principal has the power to make or break a school's culture.

There is also a misplaced view that we do not need to impose order, routine, structure or discipline in our schools. The view being that this is somewhat Victorian and draconian. In my younger years as a pupil, I cannot recall my peers reciting Shakespeare or debating educational matters as we moved from lesson to lesson. I cannot recall any of us self-regulating our behaviour or knowing better than the teacher. I can recall my peers messing around, avoiding work, punching each other and generally taking the biscuit the minute a teacher's gaze was gone and, worse still, creating flame throwers with Bunsen burners in science labs when a teacher stepped outside the lesson for too long.

If we are truly talking about social justice and reversing the Matthew Effect in our schools then children – all children – need rules, routines and boundaries and need to know what is and is *not* permissible. Without this children have no idea where they stand, what they are allowed to do and what they are not allowed to do. Without structure children will misbehave. Without certainty we all are left with uncertainty. Take driving on the roads as an example. If speed limits did not exist, if we did not have lanes or traffic lights and a clear set of rules as laid out in the Highway Code, then what would we have? I imagine chaos.

Ultimately we need to change the social norm in our schools so positive behaviour is the status quo. Children are, by their very nature, conformist. So, if the social norm within a school is to rebel, to misbehave and if nothing happens when pupils do, then guess what? More and more pupils misbehave and challenge the staff and the school's values. The quiet pupils become disaffected, disgruntled and progressively quieter and forgotten. Changing the natural state is key. As much as there is a need for rules there is also a need to make it cool to behave, to make learning the natural state.

A lot has been written about 'warm-strict' as an approach, which is an ideal Doug Lemov coined in his book *Teach Like a Champion 2.0*. Some people feel that this is a political approach, cherished by a number of right of centre advocates. Some see the word strict as worrying at best. Some feel that being strict is, once again, endorsing a Victorian approach to education. However, I would challenge this. An example of warm-strict is the daily welcome to school. I have been to many schools where staff stand at the door/gates of the school and say good morning and shake hands with every pupil as they enter the building. This is a warm, personable approach. Simultaneously, those same staff are checking for uniform infringements, picking up pupils who may have misbehaved the day before. This is the strict element and seems an entirely sensible and pro-active approach.

A major driver for improving whole-school behaviour is pro-active prevention. Nothing is ever left to chance. Far too many schools ignore this and jump straight to reactionary systems. The more that can be done within a school to prevent negative behaviours surfacing and spiralling the better. This can be achieved in a number of ways.

A key starting point for any school is to carefully consider and then cultivate the kind of culture, climate and ethos that it wants. A school's mission statement, vision and values are important but can merely be words on a page if they are not driven to be part of the very fabric of a school. As a result, leaders need to consider what kind of culture they want to cultivate, how that culture is communicated to all stakeholders and then how they teach, train and maintain that culture.

When devising a school culture it is essential to consider what your red lines are. These form your non-negotiables. In other words, they are behaviours that you simply will not tolerate. It is then important to consider an array of key questions. For example, what will you exclude for? Will you exclude? Do you have detentions? If so, are they left to teachers to direct, to departments or are they centralised? Do you have an isolation system? Do you isolate pupils in booths, isolation rooms or with senior leaders in their offices? How do you want lesson transitions to look and feel? Do you want silent corridors? Do you want line-ups? Do you have an on-call system and do you have duty/patrol staff circulating classrooms during lessons? Do you have a reward system? What do you reward pupils for? Do you want your school to be mobile phone free? How do you view punctuality to school and to lessons? Do you provide pupils with key equipment to reduce barriers to learning? What role do your tutors, if you have them, play? How are your classrooms laid out? What are the key institutional approaches?

You also need to consider whether you have rules or not. If you do, what will those rules look like? Will you have lots or a few? A key American educationalist, Marzano, cited that schools and classrooms should operate around four key rules:[3]

1. Quiet when the teacher is talking.

2. We follow directions right away.

3. We let others get on with their work.

4. We respect each other.

I personally prefer to think of things as a rule of three. Another key question, of course, is what happens when a rule is broken? What is the institutional response? How many warnings should a teacher give before a sanction is put in place? If I play devil's advocate and we insist on three warnings before a behaviour point or detention is issued then a teacher could, with a class of 30 pupils, issue 90 warnings before an actual consequence is issued. Consider for a moment just how draining that is lesson in, lesson out.

---

3. Marzano, R. J. (2005) *School Leadership That Works: From Research to Results.* Aurora, CO: Mid-continent Research for Education and Learning.

Having a clear classroom code of conduct is also important. Better still is a classroom code of conduct that is visible, in every classroom and consistently applied. In terms of the rule of three, I would personally adopt a simple trio of rules that underpin your class code of conduct, revolving around:

1. Whole-class respect and the teacher being the expert.

2. Do not distract others, with silence meaning precisely that.

3. Arrive to class punctually and fully equipped.

Naturally the wording needs to suit your school culture, vision and values but I would strongly argue that there is a need to keep things very simple, very clean and very neat.

Schools also need to teach behaviour. This does not mean just name it in an assembly and a briefing and think 'job done'. To effectively teach behaviour you have to first consider carefully what you want your school culture to be. This comes from the person at the top, who then communicates this very carefully to the governing body, then down to their senior team, middle leaders, teachers and wider staffing body. Then it needs carefully communicating to pupils, parents and any other key stakeholder. Time then needs to be taken to physically train, workshop style, everyone. This includes both staff and pupils alike.

To be able to train everyone you have to carefully design your ideal. How do you want your pupils to arrive to school, what is the morning routine, how do they enter lessons, how do they dress, how will they conduct themselves at lunch, how will they vacate the school and so on. If you want pupils to stand in lines you have to physically train them to do this. Likewise the staff to make it happen. You need to define those routines and more importantly train everyone in them. When training staff it may be useful to consider the following cycle:

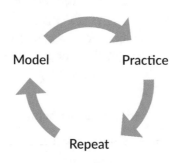

Model    Practice

Repeat

Prevention comes from routine. Routines are a behaviour that is standardised by you and carried out by staff and pupils habitually. People like routines. Routines bring about familiarity, which in turn brings about consistency and, in turn, brings about order. Once a routine is entrenched you don't have to think about the routine and how it works. Instead teachers can focus their attention on their core business, namely teaching. Pupils can then be educated and their focus can move to why they are at school, namely to learn. What is key though is that the routine for learning is consistent across a school, that it is the same from one teacher to the next. Thought needs to be given to how you want lessons to commence, where a teacher should be positioned, how the desks in your classrooms are organised.

Visibility is critical. The head needs to be a visible entity, ditto the senior team. Leading pastoral staff need to be visible. Of course, to allow for this high level of visibility something has to give. Arguably that something is irrelevant paperwork, an overkill of emails or pointless meetings. However, if senior staff are not pounding the corridors then staff are left to fend for themselves. The last thing that you want is a culture of hero teachers or teacher natural selection surfacing. If this happens, something is seriously wrong.

Visible leadership, however, needs to be supportive. Never undermine staff. If behaviour is poor this is not the teacher's fault. The teacher is not to blame. The teacher should not be vilified and the teacher should never be undermined. To do so is a game over moment.

The very best schools are metronomic in their approach. They do the same things over and over and over so that they are a habitual part of their routine, approach and culture. They become the best schools because the approach becomes an ingrained part of their culture. Visually this looks as follows:

It is also important to have sky high expectations of our pupils, which I will discuss later on within this book. It is also important to support children when they get things wrong. All children get things wrong. There has to be an approach to support, coach and mentor pupils carefully and effectively when they do fall foul. You need to consider what your approach will entail. How will you utilise tutors, pastoral staff and senior staff to provide this support? Do you appoint a designated family support worker, designated EHA co-ordinators, a counsellor, and/or a nurse to all work within your school? Do you develop an open relationship and rapport with your local police force and PCSOs? Do you create your own alternative provision? The questions surrounding behaviour, student care and how to support our pupils are endless but ultimately, as I started this chapter, a key driver in school improvement. Ignore behaviour and you ignore your biggest win.

## Final thoughts

So, to bring Chapter 3 to a close, here are the key take away points that you need to consider:

1. You need to prioritise behaviour and create a system that is pro-active and pre-emptive in design.

2. Behaviour needs to be driven from the very top down through the school.

3. We permit what we promote and we promote what we permit.

4. Behaviour should be taught, like any other curriculum-based subject.

5. Behaviour requires a lot of hard work.

# Chapter 4:
# Values and reality

## 'You permit what you promote and you promote what you permit'

### Common misconceptions

1. Respect should be earned and not automatically assumed.

2. Non-negotiables mean that you advocate a zero tolerance culture.

3. Exclusions are bad.

4. All pupils are naturally well behaved.

5. Centralising behaviour diminishes teacher authority.

In the previous chapter I posed a lot of key questions surrounding behaviour, how it should be considered, managed and responded to. In this chapter I will consider some of the key on-the-ground approaches that really do make a difference.

As a starting point I think it is pertinent to make it clear that I advocate a stance where pupils and staff should be polite, courteous, considered and nice to one another. I also advocate a stance that everyone needs to know what is expected of them, what the routines for learning are and how the average working day is structured. In my view, certainty and consistency free everyone to flourish. They rid a school of all the distractions that actually hinder learning. Subsequently, teachers are able to teach and pupils are able to learn.

I count myself lucky that as a child I had two key role models, namely my mother and father. Both emphasised the importance of remembering to say please and thank you. As Colin Firth said in *Kingsman: The Secret Service*, the 2014 movie: 'manners maketh man'. This is so true. Manners cost nothing but give everything. Having a baseline level of automatic respect for your teachers, peers and fellow pupils should be a given in schools. There are, however, some people who feel that respect has to be earned. Whilst I appreciate this stance and the logic underpinning it I still do challenge that there needs to be a baseline in place first. I would argue that rules are in place for a reason. Yes I am sure there are those who seek to bend, adapt, modify or ignore the rules but is this actually right? Rules have a purpose in a school setting, they are in place to allow everyone to learn and be safe, which are the critical fundamentals underpinning our role as educators.

I firmly believe in the notion that you permit what you promote and you promote what you permit. If you allow pupils to misbehave, then they will. If you insist on a high standard of behaviour then invariably pupils will rise to the challenge. I think it is idyllic to cite that pupils bounce from one lesson to the next discussing what they have just learnt. I am sure that some do but they are the exception not the norm. We have to change the social norm and expectations in our schools for behaviours like this to become the accepted practice. Ultimately, children need rules, they need routines, they need boundaries and they need to know what is and is not permissible. Without this children have no idea where they stand and what they are allowed or not allowed to do. Without structure children will misbehave, feel unsafe and, worse still, chaos will ensue.

A lot has been cited over the last year or so about warm-strict as an approach. It has divided teachers ideologically, with some citing that the word 'strict' in particular carries with it seriously negative connotations. I firmly advocate and believe in warm-strict as an approach. Warm-strict is nothing more than good parenting. Parents have a line that they make clear to their children, which is the strict part. As a child understands what is permissible then the warmth and love shines through. In a school setting you need both a firm set of boundaries and then really strong positive relationships. The boundaries and rules allow the relationships to grow, evolve and embed.

With this in mind I do believe that there is a need in schools to have a series of non-negotiables. These are lines in the sand that you simply will not tolerate or allow. Whilst it may sound harsh to some I do feel that these red lines should carry punitive sanctions with them, invariably either a fixed term or permanent exclusion. This may sound like a zero tolerance approach, which can bring an array of connotations with it. However, I would argue that every head and every school has its own set of behaviours and biases that it will not allow, will not condone and, subsequently, displays a degree of zero tolerance to. For example, I cannot imagine any principal addressing prospective parents and announcing that bullying and fighting are okay and will go without any form of sanction. What is absolute kryptonite in schools is low level persistent defiance, which invariably becomes a far bigger deal when left unchallenged.

The current educational climate is hugely polarised. On one side of the educational spectrum there are those who argue that exclusions, both fixed term and permanent, are inherently wrong. The argument stems around headteachers abusing their position of authority and that excluding a pupil will condemn them to a life of failure. Worse still this very pupil will join a gang and be susceptible to all sorts of wider safeguarding issues. Worse still these very heads do not care for one second about the life chances of the students that they exclude and discard any wider needs a child may have. The most devious of all heads will utilise the permanent exclusion card to enhance their exam result outcomes, timing waves of endless permanent exclusions to some sort of harmonic perfection.

It is worth highlighting that exclusion was never actually designed to be the end point for a pupil. The Local Authority, who top slice all schools a portion of their actual budget, should be providing an excluded pupil with an array of additional services to support their particular personalised needs. It also needs to be pointed out that when a school permanently excludes a pupil they often have to pay the Local Authority a fine, usually in excess of £8000. This money is to help pay for any additional services pupil X may need.

I do not believe that heads set about their day thinking, 'how many kids can I exclude today?' Heads are also teachers at the core and their moral purpose is wired to educating students to become better people ready for the 'real' world. Most heads will support a student as much as is humanly possible before ever engaging in a permanent exclusion. A lot of heads are mindful, if not scared, of excluding students. They often fear a media and/or parental backlash, they fear losing a positive Ofsted rating and/or fear, if they are part of a MAT, being criticised by the higher echelons who are seeking to keep their exclusion rates down

Many heads come under great scrutiny from their Local Authority and are forced to keep their exclusion rates down as the Local Authority themselves are chasing targets. The heads that do exclude may find that they are invited to a naughty boy/girl club to have their knuckles wrapped for excluding more students than an authority may expect or tolerate. In some cases, behaviours that would have historically warranted an exclusion are potentially brushed under the carpet and given an internal isolation or a detention as opposed to an exclusion purely because of the fear that external scrutiny and pressure brings. The reality is heads do not engage in exclusions lightly. The law pertaining to exclusions and the system of checks and balances surrounding them is so stringent that a head may as well exclude themselves than exclude a student if there is insufficient evidence in place to do so.

In terms of exclusions I do feel we should use a clear barometer test to ascertain whether an exclusion is warranted or not, namely what is considered to be an anti-social behaviour, what is outright illegal, what is wrong and what would cause us to challenge a school if our own children were subjected to it.

These are some of the behaviours that I feel serve no place in our schools:

- **Explicit swearing at staff:** I would like to be very clear here, the teacher is a figure of authority, the expert in the classroom and deserves to be respected. Nobody goes to work thinking, hoping or expecting to be sworn at. Why is a teacher any different? Why is it okay to tell a teacher to 'go forth and multiply' without consequence? In short, it is not. If you were subjected to explicit verbal abuse daily I really do doubt you would stay with your employer or profession.

- **Fighting:** Parents do not send their children to school to have someone hit them, to have someone kick them, to have someone break their nose, teeth or jaw. When a parent drops their child off at school they expect them to be 100% safe. *All* parents expect their children to be safe. Fighting has no place in society and, therefore, has no place in a school.

- **Bullying:** Bullying can bring about anxiety, a loss of self-esteem, depression, self-harming and, in its worst guise, suicide. Bullying is one of the worst forms of abuse and actually represents a safeguarding issue in its own right. Again, like fighting, parents do not send their child to school to be bullied.

- **Persistent oppositional defiance:** This simply should not be tolerated. A teacher asks a pupil to comply with an instruction. The retort, in its politest form, is 'no'. The student is asked again and again and again with the same response. This is kryptonite. This is a pupil who is very aware of what they are doing and this sort of behaviour serves no place in schools.

- **Persistent truancy:** Lessons are not optional, assembly is not optional, tutor time is not optional. I would always promote staff to find out the wider reasons behind truancy, but if there is a persistent pattern, with a student that blatantly does not care, then this needs to be addressed.

- **Smoking:** A school is a public building and smoking in a public place is, unless designated otherwise, illegal. Why then should we tolerate smoking in a school? Parents do not send their children to school to find that the toilets are littered with pupils smoking and be subjected to passive smoking.

- **Drugs, alcohol and trafficking drugs:** Drugs are illegal, that is where this begins and ends. They serve no place in society and they serve no place in schools. Trafficking drugs is a criminal offence. Likewise, pupils should not be drink or peddling alcohol. None of these behaviours serve any place or role in a school

- **Bringing a weapon into school:** Weapons serve no place in schools nor in society. We no longer live in the Medieval era where there was a need to wield a sword or axe, so why is there a need to bring a knife or a knuckle duster into school. No parent sends their child to school to be threatened by another student with a weapon.

- **Upskirting/filming or photographing a teacher or another student against their will:** Personally I agree with the view that all mobile technology should be banned in schools but these actions should not be condoned.

- **Purposefully assaulting a member of staff:** Like swearing, no member of staff in a school goes to work to be attacked. No one in any other field of work would expect a co-worker to attack them.

Heads should consider fully what support and help can be given to students to pre-empt and prevent exclusions. When a student is excluded they should consider how to help pupil X to avoid repeating that mistake again. However, all heads should have a very clear and transparent set of values and a very clear sense of what they want their school culture to feel and look like. Schools should also be a safe environment for everyone. Ultimately, parents expect their children to be as successful as they can be, to be safe and, fundamentally, to go to school for its very core purpose – to learn.

Data and statistics can be used to show its intended audience anything. A high exclusion rate could imply that a school is in chaos and has a tyrant head. A high exclusion rate could also imply that the school has standards, has high expectations, will tackle issues when they arise and will not brush them under the carpet. With the same sentiment, a low exclusion rate could mean that a school has an amazing culture but it could also mean that the school has chosen to ignore certain behaviours or disguise them with more minor sanctions to create a false sense that behaviour is positive.

I stated in the previous chapter that a clear classroom code of conduct is critical. I would ensure that your rules or expectations within a class setting are really simple, consistent across the whole-school and visible to all as an *aide-memoire*. Clear communication and over-communication is key. Consistently notifying, reminding and rehearsing the student care model and approach to all key stakeholders is an extremely powerful thing to do. Then there are no excuses for not knowing, not understanding. There is total clarity and understanding amongst all.

Classroom rules or expectations should carry with them a tiered sanction system and I firmly advocate a centralised approach to behaviour. When you expect subject teachers or heads of particular subjects to deal with behaviour and house detentions, you are not truly supporting them. Some people will, of course, cite that there is a lack of teacher autonomy here and that they do not own the behaviour. I feel this strongly misses the point. In centralising behaviour, in taking away the teacher or departmental burden away, you can really hone in on the key issues as an institution.

Centralised detentions and sanctions work. They really do. Through centralising everything an onus is placed on the senior team and pastoral staff to deal and support with behavioural issues. Teaching staff can focus on – guess what – teaching. They are safe in the knowledge that behaviour is being dealt with. This is empowering. Pupils tend to slip through the net where a school does not to operate a centralised approach to behaviour. Very often pupils are able to avoid sitting detentions or do not sit them for several weeks when a school operates a decentralised system. At its worst, a pupil who accrues multiple detentions from an array of staff often end up sitting teacher X's detention two or three weeks after the event or simply miss the detention enough times for it to be forgotten. In a centralised system this simply does not happen. Pupils quickly realise that their negative behaviour will be addressed and the silent majority, as in those who do behave, finally see that something is being done to deal with and correct negative behaviour. More importantly, it allows senior and pastoral teams to identify where patterns are emerging, where support is actually needed and to consider very carefully why some pupils may not be behaving. This is extremely powerful and, in turn, supportive to all.

With this in mind, I would argue strongly that every member of the senior team should have behaviour as part of their job description, role and remit. Gone are the days where senior teams could hide behind their office doors. Senior leaders should be visible, present, consistent and in and out of lessons. They should boss behaviour and, more importantly, support all staff. No member of staff should ever be undermined. If behaviour is poor this is not the teacher's fault. The teacher is not to blame. The teacher should not be vilified and the teacher should never be undermined. To do so is a 'game over' moment.

In any classroom the teacher is the expert. Teacher talk is fine. Direct instruction is fine. Pupils sat in rows, boy-girl, is fine. I would also promote teachers to teach with their classroom door open. This really helps to identify quickly if there is an issue and allows other staff to support a member of staff.

I would also develop a clear tutor system within a school. I am personally a huge advocate of this, with a view that each tutor serves as a mini head of year, dealing with minor issues and acting as a first port of call for parents for any minor concerns. I also feel it is important for pupils to associate themselves with one clearly distinguished member of staff, who they will see on a daily basis. This adult will serve as their in-school parent, providing pupils with support, acting as an advocate for them and, importantly, serving as a constant in their educational lives.

I would also advocate that rewarding pupils is important. Whilst we can all cite that intrinsic motivation is the most powerful form of motivation, and I appreciate the point made by those who adopt this stance, I do question this stance. We all like to be rewarded for our efforts. We all like to be told well done. As a worker I am sure we all like a pay rise when our appraisals are due. Why should this be any different for pupils? However, we must be careful what the rewards are. Saying to pupils missing tutor time, assembly or lessons is a reward is dangerous. What does this say about how we view our curriculum?

It is also really important that we support children when they get things wrong. All children get things wrong. All children make mistakes and all children will misbehave at some stage. There has to be an approach to support, coach and mentor pupils carefully and effectively when they do fall foul of our expectations and/or rules. Pupils need to be supported to learn from their mistakes and, ideally, not repeat them.

## Final thoughts

So, as this chapter comes to a close here are the key take away points for you to ponder:

1. Every single school has some behaviours that it simply will not condone. All heads, whether they admit it or not, have zero tolerance to certain actions.

2. Low level persistent defiance is kryptonite to a classroom and school culture.

3. Exclusions are necessary to keep our school communities safe.

4. Exclusion was never designed to be the end. The issue is one of funding at a Local Authority level for appropriate alternative provision.

5. Every single school suffers from poor pupil behavioural choices at some stage.

6. Be wary of what the data surrounding behaviour says. Is it really telling you the whole truth?

# Section 3:

## The curriculum is God

# Chapter 5:
# The importance
# of knowledge

## 'Knowledge itself is power'

### Common misconceptions

1. A knowledge rich approach is solely about rote learning for pub quizzes.

2. *We* have always taught knowledge.

3. Data is more important than knowledge and student progress can be tracked via a flight path.

4. Spiralling the curriculum down from GCSE to Year 7 leads to academic success.

5. Skills are transferable and mean the same thing to all subject domains.

The role, place and importance of knowledge within the curriculum has taken something of a bashing throughout my career. When I undertook my PGCE subject knowledge sat on the highest of all pedestals. As a trainee you had to know your subject inside out, you had to be extremely well versed and well read. The pre-reading list prior to starting my PGCE course contained more books than a little. I read them all, not because I wanted to be the best or to show off but because I realised that knowledge itself is power. Sadly the place and importance of knowledge seemed to be secondary once I moved from my PGCE into the 'real world'. A classic argument is that 'we have always taught knowledge'. I am sure we have but it is the emphasis on knowledge that has been weathered. A skills-driven focus over the course of a decade has been viewed in favour of the use of knowledge.

During the early stages of my career Bloom's Taxonomy was peddled in schools. It was regularly cited that the National Curriculum of the early 2000s was founded upon Bloom. Bloom itself places a heavy emphasis on the role of skills, such as analysis, synthesis and evaluation. The inference has been that knowledge, recall and comprehension are less challenging. This greatly shaped the way teachers delivered, or were expected to deliver, lessons for a good decade. A surge of cross-curricular skills were pushed in schools, knowledge dropped further and further down the pecking order and teachers were expected to entertain pupils, with pacey lessons, learning styles, group work, VAK questionnaires, card sorts and so on.

Knowledge was further debased with a view that data was king, that learning is linear and that we can track a pupil's performance via the imposition of a flight path. Flight paths have assumed that a child will make a full grade of progress from one year to the next. So, for example, Pupil X enters your school in Year 7 on the equivalence of a 2, by Year 8 they will be on a 3, Year 9 a 4, Year 10 a 5 and by the end of Year 11 a 6. I have sign data systems that flash red, amber and green if pupils were not making the necessary sub-level of progress from one term to the next. The assumption of these flawed models is that learning is linear. Learning is *not* linear. To assume so is to assume that humans learn like robots and have system upgrades. This is simply not the case. We all flourish with certain topics and find others far more challenging. Learning is more like a giant rollercoaster, with ups and downs.

Flight paths have also promoted a false and flawed sense that the GCSE exam at the end is everything. This has promoted schools to take the

GCSE content, assessment criteria and specifications and spiral them downwards, all the way into Year 7. I have seen so many schools adopt spiralled curriculums, with GCSE number grades employed in Year 7. Year 7 pupils have been trained to speak in GCSE language. Key Stage 3 has been redacted to two years in length in some settings, all in favour of a longer GCSE experience. In effect, some schools have become exam factories. Where, within this approach, is the wider sense of learning, the broad and balanced curriculum? Again a misconception is the notion that broad and balanced means delivering hundreds of subjects. It does not. It means allowing the learning to flow, prioritising knowledge, allowing pupils to explore the content, to make mistakes, to learn from them. It is about truth and the wider pursuit of truth and knowledge as a whole. It is to be free of the shackles imposed by a data driven curriculum, expecting a sub-level of progress every term.

A further flaw in our education system has been the drive on skills. The assumption that skills are transferable from one subject to the next. Whilst I would advocate that literacy and numeracy are key bedrocks to the curriculum, I would also argue that these two distinct areas of knowledge are just that, knowledge. They are keys, of course, to a pupil's ability to access and comprehend the wider curriculum but they are not skills.

The employment of PLTs, thinking skills days, leadership challenges, resilience learning, PLCs and many other skill orientated approaches makes a wild assumption, namely that concepts such as evaluation or analysis can be taught in their own distinct right and applied to the curriculum as a whole. This is an extremely lazy narrative and another case of searching for a silver bullet. The ability to analyse, evaluate and synthesise ideas in PE will vary wildly to history, to geography, to maths. How can a thinking skills day focusing on a cross-transferability of skills make one a better historian? One's ability to interpret and evaluate why World War One began comes from understanding the root causes of the war, the core facts, the historical narrative and historiographical interpretations. It does not come from a wider view that today we had an assembly on how to evaluate and you can apply this to any subject.

When we talk about cross-curricular links what is really meant is knowledge that can cross the subject flooring. For example, knowledge via RE about Christianity and Catholicism will help a pupil as a framework to understand the Reformation movement. However, the way in which an RE specialist and a history teacher would evaluate this historical event will be different.

A key issue with education is arguing that knowledge unlocks everything sounds almost boring. It does not sound as exciting as let's let the pupils loose on an ICT room, research in groups about the context of *The Iliad*, present this back to one another and record an iMovie. The issue though is the seductive nature of excitement often does not lead to deep-rooted learning. The reality is that learning is hard, learning can be difficult, learning can be challenging and the pursuit of knowledge can be taxing. Add to that that learning is not linear and you can see where frustrations around why the pupils are not making rapid progress, why the pupils are not going up a level, we need to visibly see the learning and so on. In reality, learning is not visible. Teaching may well be but learning is not.

## Final thoughts

As this chapter comes to a close, here are some of the key points to consider:

1. Subject knowledge is king and knowledge itself is power.

2. A skills-rich approach, based on pace, has weathered away the importance of knowledge and the agency of the curriculum.

3. Learning is not linear and it is foolhardy to think so. Therefore, progress is not linear.

4. Skills are not transferable. Skills come from the subject specific domain knowledge.

# Chapter 6:
# The curriculum is a progression model

## 'The King is dead, long live the King'

### Common misconceptions

1. The curriculum, and thinking about the curriculum, is secondary to pacey lesson activities.

2. Knowledge nullifies skills.

3. The Matthew Effect will be fixed by teaching 21$^{st}$ century skills.

4. High speed curriculums, that fast track pupils to Key Stage 4, lead to positive academic outcomes.

The curriculum is a major school improvement driver. It is the very essence and heartbeat of a school. It is critical that we ensure our curricular design is robust to give all pupils, including the most disadvantaged, the very best life chances possible. It is also the key to unlocking and reversing the Matthew Effect. I also strongly adhere to a view that pupils need to know stuff or, as E. D. Hirsch said, 'knowledge begets knowledge'. Knowledge is therefore fertile. Taken another step further, you simply cannot think critically without knowledge. What exactly are you attempting to analyse, evaluate, synthesise and so on if you do not possess deep-rooted disciplinary knowledge.

The curriculum is entwined within a whole-school ethos and is just as critical and important as the approaches to assessment, student care, behaviour and discipline. The curriculum defines the tone of the school and, in some respects, sets the heartbeat and rhythm of the school.

Over the last two years the idea of a knowledge-based curriculum has surfaced and, in many regards, become the phrase of the day. The critics cite that this approach loses sight of the skills that pupils need to be successful learners, many of which are deemed to be transferable from one subject to the next. Some critics cite that a knowledge bias is simply turning education into a pub quiz factory, with pupils merely learning by rote. However, I would argue that pupils simply need to know stuff. More eloquently, 'knowledge begets knowledge.' I firmly take the view that we cannot believe our pupils have the assumed subject and wider knowledge already. It is our role to give them the knowledge that they need to succeed.

Personally I never want to hear the phrase 'but the students do not possess the necessary cultural capital to succeed'. Whilst this may be true, may be the case and may be founded, the reality is it is our job as the teachers to support this overall development of cultural capital in our students. If we wave a white flag and do not do it, who will? That is why the content is king and why knowledge is the queen that reigns with divine right across the curriculum. Knowledge itself is power and without knowledge, and just skills, our students are left simply with nothing. Therefore there needs to be clarity regarding what is taught and why.'

The clarity of thought behind the curriculum is critical. This serves as a road-map, directing both the teacher and the student to the halcyon dream of a knowledge rich wonderland. Underpinning this are a number of key questions to consider, namely:

- What will a student know by the end of a Key Stage? Why?
- What will a student know by the end of this year? Why?
- What will a student know by the end of this term? Why?

- What will a student know by the end of this week? Why?
- What will a student know by the end of this lesson? Why?
- What is the substantive knowledge students need to know? Why?
- What is the disciplinary knowledge students need to know? Why?

If we take these key questions a step further then we need to carefully consider whether our curriculum in its fullest sense and at a subject level drives the school's purpose. Whether it matches the school's vision. Whether it challenges pupils, builds sufficient background knowledge to allow all pupils to succeed, has a clear idea of the big ideas and ideals you want to achieve as a school. Is it fit for your contextual setting and promotes the sequential building of knowledge. Ultimately, does the curriculum promote pupils to search for the truth and allow them to develop a sense of academic justice. Further questions to consider include:

- Does the curriculum demonstrate that there is high ambition for all students?

- Is the curriculum broad and balanced? In particular, do all students have full access to the full national curriculum programmes of study in all subjects in Key Stage 3?

- Are any adaptations made to the curriculum for SEND and the most disadvantaged students?

- Have the subject leaders assured and ensured appropriate and logical content choices and sequencing? Does curriculum planning help students to remember and know more, over time?

- To what extent is there an all-through curriculum intent across subjects?

- To what extent is assessment in all its forms effective?

Key to the strength of the curriculum are high expectations and no excuses. We need to be wary of perpetually making excuses for our pupils. Comments such as 'these pupils never amount to much' or 'they won't get it' or 'they lack the cultural awareness to ever understand' are poisonous, inhibiting and ultimately suffocating.

Dylan Wiliam said 'if you don't know where you're going, you'll never get there.'[4] This really resonates with me when I think hard and deep about the curriculum. You have to know what you want your students to learn, when and why. Teachers need to know what they want their students to understand. Lessons, sequences of lessons and schemes of work need to be carefully planned, carefully sequenced, have a clear purpose and place within the wider broader curricular design.

As Clare Sealy cited at a ResearchED convention, the curriculum 'is like a boxset. It should contain "sub plots" (resolved in one lesson), "main plots" (resolved in one topic) and a "story arc" resolved over years.' Doug Lemov said 'perhaps the single most powerful way to bring efficiency, focus and rigour to a classroom is by installing strong procedures and routines.'[5]

Teacher subject knowledge is also key to ensuring the relative success of the enacted curriculum. As the Sutton Trust report states, 'great teaching comes from a teachers' content knowledge, including the ability to understand how students think about a subject and identify common misconceptions (and) quality of instruction, which includes using strategies like effective questioning and the use of assessment.' A key question, therefore, is how do you privy subject knowledge? If we build further on that question, what is the relationship between a teacher and the knowledge that they teach?

It is important to consider the substantive, core, disciplinary knowledge that we want our pupils to learn (i.e. the facts), just as much as we should consider the disciplinary knowledge that we want our pupils to learn (i.e. what is up for grabs). Through the enacted curriculum we need to consider carefully what we, as teachers, are doing in the classroom and what we want our pupils to do.

This then brings us to the use of knowledge organisers. Some have seen these as a silver bullet that allows you to virtue signal that your curriculum is knowledge rich. After all, you have a document that has bullet pointed the knowledge you want your pupils to know. I prefer to think of knowledge organisers as a bible guide to a unit of work. In my

4. Wiliam, D. (2011) *Embedded Formative Assessment*. Bloomington, IN: Solution Tree Press.
5. Lemov, D. (2015) *Teach Like a Champion 2.0*. San Francisco, CA: Jossey-Bass.

opinion all pupils should have one given to them for every new topic of work that they study for every subject. However, I feel that they should serve to act as a manual, as much as they do an organiser. I would advocate formulating knowledge organisers that do the following:

- Have the theme for the term (for example The Causes of World War One)
- Have the Big Questions for the term as a contents page
- Where applicable have a sample of an assessment the pupil may face, coupled with the assessment criteria and a good sample answer
- Contain the homework for the half term
- Contain a list of books for wider reading
- Then contain the actual organiser itself

What is key is that the organiser is not simply a bolt on gimmick. It has to be built into your enacted curriculum and routinely used as part of your lesson delivery. Otherwise the organiser is tokenistic.

I deliberately referenced homework and there are many thoughts on the role and merits of setting homework. Personally I do feel homework develops good habits in pupils. I would, however, set homework that lends itself well to retrieval practice. The best homework is where a pupil has to read and memorise a piece of academic text. This can then be picked up on within the enacted curriculum in the form of low stakes retrieval quizzes, which are self or peer marked. This ultimately helps to support the development of a pupil's long-term schema.

Where knowledge organisers are used well they can form a vital reference point for both staff and pupils, clearly labelling the powerful knowledge that underpins learning, knowledge organisers can reduce cognitive load, leading to automaticity. They are also key to supporting the most disadvantaged pupils who are likely to not have the background knowledge and wider awareness of the more advantaged pupil. They can also be used effectively for self-quizzing and developing a pupil's wider vocabulary and command of the literacy. Where knowledge organisers are most effective are where they are built into the enacted curriculum, therefore utilised daily.

I do feel it is important for every subject area to have its own set of schemes of work, curriculum design plans and a curriculum intent overview. In failing to do this we are leaving things as a profession to chance. This is not about bending the knee to a new Ofsted framework, rather this is about astute and in-depth curricular planning. If we do not know what we want our pupils to learn, when to learn it, why we want them to learn it and how, then I would argue we have a problem. If we live day by day, lesson by lesson, by the seat of our pants, never really truly understanding the bigger picture then our pupils will never meet their full potential.

We also need to take our time with the curriculum. Why have we, in recent years, rushed Key Stage 3 and redacted it to a two-year exercise, with pupils making their GCSE options at the end of Year 7. This has simply served to negate the agency of the curriculum. It has prohibited pupils and teachers from exploring the wider fruits of the curriculum as a whole and – at its crudest – turned schools into exam factories churning out pupils who are anything but knowledge rich.

We need to carefully consider the powerful knowledge we want our pupils to have access to and where breadth and depth are needed. We also need to consider where oracy plays a part, where we promote academic reading and where and how we do or do not build in assessments. Ultimately all of the decisions that we have to make with regards to the curriculum are high stakes, requiring extreme thought and reasoning. Social justice is at stake and this cannot be taken lightly.

## Final thoughts

As this chapter comes to a close, some key musings for you include:

1. Pupils simply need to know stuff (knowledge) to access the curriculum and learn.

2. Without knowledge pupils are left with nothing, thus turbo charging the Matthew Effect.

3. The curriculum is like a story and should have a clear beginning, middle and end.

4. The curriculum is an agency in itself and an extremely powerful school improvement driver and force for justice.

# Section 4:

## The teacher is the expert

# Chapter 7:
# Teaching, teaching, teaching

## The guide from the side!

### Common misconceptions

1. Pupils retain over 80-90% of what they teach one another.

2. Teachers need to serve as facilitators of learning.

3. Learning objectives facilitate learning.

Around ten years ago I first heard the phrase 'the guide from the side'. This came in to play as part of an era promoting the notion that the pupils in our classrooms needed to teach themselves. Research cited that pupils learnt and retained the most information when they, not the teacher, taught one another. In my opinion, what this approach and ideal missed was that most pupils lacked the necessary base of knowledge to be able to teach one another. That teachers would waste many hours teaching pupils again to iron out misconceptions that Google and Wikipedia had taught them.

The notion that a teacher is an entertainer and facilitator first and an imparter of knowledge second is beyond the pale of my understanding. It is no wonder that many schools engage fully in the circus of intervention as soon as the turnbuckle of Year 11 begins because students have not learnt as much as they should have done in the previous four years. When was it thought that a student who knows very little about a topic should help to mentor and co-teach another student who knows equally very little about the subject. The other cliché is that the bright capable student in the classroom should support the least able student as this will help the latter. Is this not the job of the teacher and will this not hold the 'brighter' student back from making even more progress with their own learning? Yet in an era of PLTS, APP, AFL, WALT, WILF, MUST-SHOULD-COULD, facilitative learning and marking every word to within an inch of its life that was the Holy Grail. That was what made Outstanding, coupled with an ability to do cartwheels and entertain the masses.

When we pose the question which teacher did you respect the most and why the responses usually revolve around a teacher that was strict, inspiring and, importantly, knowledgeable. When I was a pupil my history and geography teachers were awe inspiring. Why? Both had the same approach to teaching and both had a similar style. They would always welcome my class, as they did every class, at the door, asking how we were on entry. There was always a focus question, which was the lesson title, on the board. We knew, simply because it had been drilled into us, that we would be answering that question in the lesson. However, what made these teachers so special was that they knew their subject like the back of their hand. Almost half of the lesson would entail imparting their knowledge onto us, the empty vessels, whilst we made copious notes, were questioned (very carefully) and had our learning expertly scaffolded.

I am very clear about the approach I want to see. Like my old history and geography teachers I want to see staff welcoming students at the doors of classrooms, giving students a retrieval quiz to undertake as a settler. All lessons should have a clear hook, i.e. a *big question*. Students and the teacher know that this is the lesson focus, which also serves as the lesson title in exercise books. There is, therefore, no need for hours of agonising over every word that goes into every lesson objective under the sun. There is no need for the students to waste 10 to 15 minutes copying down objectives that mean next to nothing to them but that they can recite parrot-like fashion just in case a visitor comes in and asks 'so what are the lesson objectives for your class today?' Never was there a greater false proxy for learning than students retorting positively to that question.

Furthermore, the teacher is the expert. The teacher is the one who imparts the knowledge. The teacher is the one who has spent hundreds of hours expanding their subject knowledge, refining their pedagogical craft and crafting the overall plan for the lesson. If the teacher is not the expert, if the teacher is to serve as agent facilitator, then why bother with subject specialist teachers. In fact, why bother with a teacher at all?

I am firm in my view that there is nothing wrong with a teacher delivering a mini lecture, framing a lesson around carefully crafted higher order questions, engaging pupils in low stakes retrieval quizzes and mini-tests. Teachers should also be given the freedom, time and space to read academic texts with their pupils and help the pupils to comprehend the meaning of such texts. Pupils should be actively encouraged to make notes too.

Teaching, it seems to me, has been made out to be a complex beast. Please do not incorrectly quote me here. Teaching is a hard job that requires a lot of hard work, commitment, dedication and incredible subject knowledge. Teachers over the last two decades have been expected to produce 30 different worksheets for 30 different students all measured against multiple lesson objectives. Everything has been geared in the last decade to entertaining students and sending them on bogus voyages of discovery. There is also the data driven view that students learn in a linear fashion and make progress in a vertical line. If your class are not doing this then you are failing as a teacher. There is no sense within this that the student may be responsible for their learning or that learning is actually almost impossible to measure. Humans, however, do not make perfect progress in an upward trajectory. We all struggle with aspects of our learning.

In short, let the teacher teach. Let their subject specialist knowledge flow through and into their students. Do not limit expectations on students with a false sense that 30 differentiated objectives and worksheets means progress. I am not convinced that it does. The teacher is not a 'learning designer', a 'facilitator' nor an 'entertainer.' A teacher is precisely that, a teacher. Do not lose sight of what an art it is to be a teacher.

## Final thoughts

As this chapter draws to a close some of the key points to ponder include:

1. The teacher is the expert and should be treated as such.

2. Clear routines for learning are key to learning.

3. Learning objectives waste time, serving as white noise in a classroom setting and a false proxy for learning.

4. Teacher subject knowledge is critical.

# Chapter 8:
# Keeping it simple

## Learning objectives and differentiation: Rabbit hole or useful?

### Common misconceptions

1. Differentiation by task supports pupil learning and pupil progress.

2. You need to differentiate your lesson to be 'Outstanding'.

3. Pupils rehearsing and reciting lesson objectives is a sign that learning is taking place.

4. Being busy in the classroom, with lots of lesson activities, means learning is deep.

Differentiation has a unique dual effect of consuming hundreds of teacher hours in planning and preparation in a vague hope of supporting pupils to make progress and, simultaneously capping expectations on pupils, therefore inhibiting their progress. My view is that all pupils should have access to the same content, the same powerful knowledge and have the same expectations placed upon them. Nothing says I do not believe in you more than a learning activity that is notably different to the rest of the class, such as the green worksheet, with the 'fill in the gap' exercise. In short, I would argue that the term differentiation should be abolished and banned in our schools. At best it causes confusion regarding its actual meaning.

Some people will cite that scaffolding, tiered and strategically utilised questions and personalised one-to-one support are all forms of differentiation. They may well be but the confusion surrounding what the term differentiation actually means is less than helpful. I would argue that we should call the strategies and approaches that we do utilise in our lessons by their actual name (i.e. scaffolding, questioning, personalised support and so on) and not place them under some grey umbrella term. Differentiation as a term has been lazily used as a form of lesson observation feedback too. How many times has lesson feedback taken the form of 'you needed to differentiate your lesson more?' What does this actually mean? I imagine that even the observer giving the feedback could not truly answer this question with any real degree of clarity and precision.

I also advocate removing lesson or learning objectives from lesson delivery. Teachers can use them as part of their overall planning but I would argue that the employment of a must/should/could set of learning objectives in a lesson is less than helpful and, again, caps expectations. Throughout my career I have found the use of 'Big Questions' far more powerful and far more helpful. They are an approach that can be used across all disciplines.

As with all things in education it is fair to ask questions of an approach. Some key questions that I would use to challenge the use of Big Questions include:

- Are they a fad?
- Where is the research to back up the claim that this approach works?
- Does it restrict teaching?
- Is it possible some questions will end up poorly written?
- Why would you roll them out whole-school?
- What is the opportunity cost of using them?

In essence a Big Question is a hook for a lesson or sequence of lessons. Their effective use encourages pupils to explore a problem, drawing on substantive subject-specific knowledge. If they are used effectively then they will bring about a neat interplay of the core (the stuff/knowledge) that pupils need to know and the hinterland (stories, frames and hooks) upon which to hang that core disciplinary knowledge. If anything, they are integral to a knowledge-rich approach. If I were to pose a challenging Big Question to my class, for example, 'how significant was the role of propaganda in Hitler's rise to power?' then I am going to draw upon a very clever interplay of long-term knowledge (what is in the pupils' schema) and present brand new material. This material will then be carefully presented, scaffolded and modelled. Effective questioning will be employed to really draw out pupil learning. The ultimate aim is that the pupils can produce an end product. In this example, I am also coaxing my pupils to consider a deeper subject specific disciplinary skill i.e. to consider 'how far'. This is by no means easy and is a highly sophisticated thing to do. However, is this really unique to just history?

The use of 'Big Questions' is not new. The history community have employed their use for many years and they are integral to effective history teaching. As Christine Counsell once said: 'Enquiry is more than pupils finding out – they do something with what they discover. It is a coherent learning sequence (single lesson or unit of work) exploring a historical problem or question drawing upon at least one distinctive area of disciplinary thinking. It is our way of shaping the historical thinking we want pupils to do.'[6] Ian Luff wrote: 'In answering an enquiry question pupils necessarily demonstrate their understanding of substantive concepts as they construct increasingly sophisticated arguments to justify their claims.'[7] Big Questions, therefore, structure learning, they help to teach second order concepts and the use of the question helps with the delivery and teaching of substantive knowledge. They help to make knowledge sticky.

Yes, the history community have championed the use of 'Big Questions'. Yes, they work highly effectively in history. However, they are a major

---

6. Cited by McFahn, R. (2016) 'Using enquiry to succeed at 9-1 GCSE history', *History Resource Cupboard* [Online] 25 October. Retrieved from: www.bit.ly/2toQ2Ay
7. Luff, I. (2016) 'Cutting the Gordian Knot: taking control of assessment', *Teaching History* 164 pp. 38-46.

open secret. My challenge is why can other subjects not adopt these too? Why would other subjects not want to take an approach that one curricular discipline has championed and make it their own? If it works in one academic area of the curriculum, why would it not elsewhere? The reality is they can and do. Yes, they take time, care and careful consideration. However, that is the case for all effective teaching and all of the strategies that we employ. If we give something careful thought, plan it well and execute it accordingly it invariably works. If we don't we tend to find that things flop. Knowledge organisers are a prime example here. They can be disastrous or brilliant. However, if they are brilliantly used I wouldn't want them contained to just one disciplinary area when they are applicably useful across the whole spectrum. What is key, however, is that they are made subject specific.

In terms of opportunity cost, the formation of learning objectives, the creation of the slide detailing them and the lost learning time in copying them down is simply not worth it. Teacher time is criminally wasted, as is pupil time and learning objectives are a false proxy that learning is taking place. Learning objectives are often like a comfort blanket wrapping a school in a false sense of being busy equals learning. Big Questions, by comparison, prioritise knowledge and remove a lot of fluff. Some Big Questions can span multiple lessons. Some lessons do not need them. Some lessons are pause lessons. Some lessons are assessment based. Staff can use their own professional judgement.

Much of my thinking has been underpinned through reading the works of a number of key educationalists. Firstly, Doug Lemov's *Teach Like A Champion 2.0* is a book that I rate highly. I strongly believe in routines for learning. Routines create consistency, allow staff to think more sharply about their disciplinary knowledge and the actual efficacy of teaching. As Doug Lemov states: 'perhaps the single most powerful way to bring efficiency, focus and rigor to a classroom is by installing strong procedures and routines. You define a right way to do recurring tasks; you practice doing them with students so they roll like clockwork. This applies at least as much to "academic" tasks as it does to more procedural ones.' With this in mind the adoption of the 'Big Questions' becomes part of the class-based routine for learning,

Pupils ultimately like routines, they build positive security and allow the learning to take place.

Dylan Wiliam has said: 'if you don't know where you're going, you'll never get there'.[8] In other words, what do we want students to know and be able to do? How do we clarify, share and understand learning intentions. As with all things, keep it simple! If we have layers of intentions or objectives in a lesson then we all become lost. The white noise created by this information overload is deafening. The use of a 'Big Question' simplifies this considerably. There is one big focal question and everyone knows what they are aspiring to achieve. There is no confusion. This resonates with Rosenshine's 'Principles of Instruction' around sequencing concepts, providing models and appropriate scaffolding. Big Questions lend themselves well to Rosenshine, which is an approach adopted by a number of schools as a vehicle for structuring lessons.

I would even subscribe to some of the points made by Hattie. Hattie said: 'that targeted lessons have a positive impact on student attainment. This does not mean learning objectives. What this means is, teachers knowing what they want students to understand within a given time frame.'[9] Subsequently, lessons need to be carefully planned, carefully sequenced, have a clear purpose and a place within the wider scheme of work. Again, Big Questions can allow this to happen. As mentioned previously, Clare Sealy has been quoted as saying: 'a curriculum should contain "sub plots" (resolved in one lesson), "main plots" (resolved in one topic) and a "story arc" resolved over years.' I would argue that those sub plots, main plots and the full story can all take the form of 'Big Questions,' providing a sound peg to hang all of the core knowledge you need pupils to know on to.

Staff need to carefully consider what they want to achieve in lesson X; how this links to lesson Y; how this links to next weeks, months and years learning. Bringing about a philosophical change by moving from learning objectives to 'Big Questions' will encourage staff to really consider the curriculum as a progression model. Introducing staff to the concept of 'Big Questions', asking them to consider how this could work

8. Lemov, D. (2015) *Teach Like a Champion 2.0.* San Francisco, CA: Jossey-Bass.
9. Hattie, J. (2008) *Visible Learning.* Abingdon, Oxon: Routledge.

for them and giving them the time to truly consider the curriculum as a whole is anything but sloppy thinking. Promoting staff to think about the intent and enactment of their curriculum in a deeper, richer and more meaningful manner is never a bad thing.

## Final thoughts

As this chapter comes to a close, you may wish to ponder on the following key take away points:

1. Differentiation destroys expectations and places a glass ceiling on pupil progress.

2. Differentiation is ill defined, ill understood and creates a suffocating fog of confusion in schools.

3. Learning objectives are often poorly thought out, time consuming and do not lend themselves to pupil progress.

4. Big Questions promote pupils to draw on substantive subject specific knowledge, which aids pupil understanding of both the core and the hinterland.

# Section 5:

## Workload matters

# Chapter 9:
# Protecting staff

## Rationalising teacher workload

### Common misconceptions

1. Teaching should hurt.

2. Teachers need to be in at 7am and should not leave until at least 6pm.

3. Teachers need to regulate their own workload and any attempt to do so by SLT is to stifle free choice.

4. Planning is a skill that should be mastered in isolation.

5. Being busy means you are effective.

6. Lots of emails mean a good job is being performed and everyone understands.

How often as a teacher have you felt that sleep is a luxury? If you can just squeeze in another hour of work, mark a few more books, plan another lesson, respond to a few more emails, then your day tomorrow will be just that little bit easier. Over time, however, you begin to burn the candle at both ends, becoming jaded, ill and, at the very worst, burnt out. This in turn causes people to leave the profession despite having shown so much potential and promise as a trainee teacher. The notion that teachers work from 9am to 3pm and have 13 weeks off a year is a fallacy.

I would like to iron out a fact; teaching is not an easy profession. It never has been and it probably never will be. I liken teaching to having to serve as a stand-up comic for five or six hours a day, five days a week, plus all of the extra work that has to be done in your own time. The key difference though is that no one would expect a stand-up to go on tour and perform a five to six hour set daily. I have seen people describe some teachers as martyrs or that they should be able to regulate their own workload. To some extent this may be true. However, I do see it as the responsibility of senior leaders, especially the Head, in their 'magic ivory tower,' to do something to rationalise staff workload.

I do believe a lot can be done to support staff with unnecessary workload demands. Whilst the basic premise of the job is unlikely to change anytime soon, namely that the job demands intense bursts of energy, there is a lot that can be done to alleviate pressure on us all.

Firstly, and I would argue that this is a big sticking point, is to avoid and resist fads. Fads are seductive and sometimes come across as the magic silver bullet. In reality, are they? I prefer to keep things simple and focused. To my mind everything should come back to your School Improvement Plan (SIP). If it is not on the SIP, if it has not been communicated out in a timely fashion, then do not do it.

With this in mind, keep things simple. Whilst it is now accepted that there is no preferred learning style I would make it clear that direct instruction is a credible approach within the classroom. I would also emphasise that classes can work in silence, that pupils can make notes or being lectured. Big lectures can be used to support the learning of pupils. Equally we can cut staff a lot of slack by not insisting on learning objectives in lessons. Teachers spend hundreds of hours agonising over objectives, the style, format, wording, making the PowerPoint that contains them to look corporate. To what effect? Who did the objectives actually help and satisfy? Personally, I do not want to ever walk into a classroom to see students writing down the endless array of objectives into their books and killing off 10 to 15 minutes of teaching time again. With the same token, do we need to differentiate learning through the use of 30 different coloured worksheets that are all specially formatted to meet the needs of each and every single pupil? Often this form of differentiation serves to cap expectations on pupils, causing more harm than good and a lot of wasted teacher time.

Co-planning is another critical approach. If department X has ten teachers and each of them are teaching Year 7 tomorrow period one, do we really want those members of staff going home tonight to plan ten separate lessons for period one tomorrow? What is the cost-benefit analysis here? I would argue that a far sounder use of staff time is to support teams to work together to co-plan schemes of work, lesson content and lesson resources. Yes, you can personalise things for your pupils but you do not need to individually reinvent the wheel. Ten teachers planning the same lesson individually, at say a conservative one hour per teacher, is a lot of time lost.

Emails are my first sticking point. Most emails are a waste of time. Most emails are trash and very few actually warrant our attention. However, the negative psychological pressure of knowing you have 50 emails in your inbox is impossible to measure. When an email stretches much beyond one or two paragraphs it really warrants a face-to-face discussion. At one stage in my career I used to receive 350 emails a day. There has to be a point where we say *enough is enough*. Heads can support this by changing the institutional culture. They can bring in email embargoes at weekends and holidays. This approach really does work. We can prevent the whole-staff circular emails of pupil X has lost their pen. The key to restricting email use is to ensure that staff have sufficient face-to-face directed time to meet and discuss items in person. It also helps when the senior team themselves agree core messages and send out only one or two missives a week, rather than hundreds of emails.

Giving staff time is key. Within the context of any one given half term you can organise your meeting schedules as a school to allow year teams to meet weekly, to allow departments to meet four or five times a half term. A key question here is, how many whole-staff meetings do you actually need? Can you change the format of your weekly staff briefing so that the focus is a weekly short and sharp 15-minute long staff training session instead? This then allows middle leaders the time to drive the curriculum, their subject, their staff's subject knowledge and so on. In other words, deal with the really important stuff that actually matters to them.

Within any one given academic year we have five key training days' worth of time to work with. How do you use this? Do you go for a combination of INSET days and Twilights or just INSETs? Do you afford staff traded days? How do you carve this time up decisively between the corporate whole-school agenda and the needs of departments X, Y and Z? Another thing we can do is to give faculties away days for planning. If we collectively agree to cover one another we can buy each department two days undisturbed in the second half of the summer term to plan, build up resources, schemes of work and so on.

With faculty away days in mind I would advocate schools avoiding roll-over. I have worked in schools that used to roll their calendar forward at May half term. Subsequently, gained time became a thing of the past. This puts staff under undue pressure and does not allow you, the school or the staff, the adequate air time and space to prepare for the new academic year. This time can be constructively used to work on the new curricular approach and to provide staff with vital training.

Data is another key area. I have worked in settings with flight paths, six data captures a year and four sets of mock exams over the GCSE and Post 16 cycle. I have also seen data spreadsheets printed every six weeks, with the view that we need to measure progress at light speed. Why? Can we not reduce the number of data drops in our schools to two or three a year? How many mock exams do we really need to put our pupils through? There is a real danger that we are simply weighing the pig with endless mock examinations and not embedding learning. At its worst, endless mocks just affirm and reaffirm to some pupils that they are likely to fail and then a sense of 'what is the point?' creeps in. Added to that, who is actually marking these endless mock exams? What thought has gone into when they take place? Why? For what purpose? The same can be said for data. What exactly is it that we want to measure and why? What is it that we actually want to report on to parents and why? A lot can be done here to reduce workload, increase the time actually devoted to learning and, importantly, support pupil outcomes more fruitfully.

I have already spoken about behaviour earlier on within this book but centralising behaviour and having a clear set of routines for learning really is a time saver all round. With the same token, can revision sessions be rationalised so that they do not begin for Year 11 and Year 13 on the 5th of September after school? Operating a Period 6 revision culture, spanning ten months of the year, sounds great on paper and highly supportive of the pupils. However, this approach adds hundreds of additional hours to staff workload over the course of the academic year and the overall attendance to Period 6 sessions is often variable. Equally Year 11 and Year 13 pupils will not maintain the level of revision intensity you desire for ten months of the year. They will, however, see the relevance and importance of a ten-week rundown to the exams.

Marking is another key area where we can make huge time savings for staff. Why do we insist on marking everything, scrawling books with red pen until the ink runs out, writing extensive lengthy prose in the hope that a pupil will read it, understand the comments, reflect and then action them. Worse still are approaches such as what went well and even better if, followed by a DIRT task. The reality is most pupils will struggle to comprehend fully what has been written in their books as most of the language used will be in teacher talk. The feedback will have taken hours for teacher X to produce and then invaluable lesson time is often wasted asking pupils to write a DIRT answer to a question they have already struggled to do with little to no guidance. Whole-class feedback is a far more impactful approach to marking. It takes little time, with the majority of the feedback given to pupils in class as part of the overall lesson delivery. Staff time is far better utilised skimming over pupil books looking for common points to celebrate, common misconceptions and clear areas that need to be taught again. If every pupil has misspelt a key term why correct it in every single book. The feedback should take place in class.

One of the biggest time savers for all staff is to resist fads as they come at us in real time. Stick to your school improvement plan priorities for the year. Do not change, change and change again the direction of travel in your school every two minutes. This brings about uncertainty, inconsistency and, worse still, a sense that you do not know what you are doing. It is also important to give staff time to reflect, consider and then plan for any changes you are seeking to make. I often feel it is worth signposting to staff what will be coming in September in January. This gives staff eight to nine months to get their head around this. How many times have we heard a head announce that they want something to happen as of tomorrow, without training, clarity, thought or direction? It merely comes at us a directive from nowhere. This is an approach to avoid like the plague.

## Final thoughts

As this chapter draws to a close, some points for you to ponder:

1. Heads/SLT can do a lot to support staff with their workload.

2. Stick to your school improvement plan, do not deviate direction.

3. Work as a team; co-plan, establish subject communities and upskill one another.

4. Give staff the time, space and freedom to undertake their core job, namely teaching.

5. Giving subject areas the lion's share of directed time does not mean you are a poor or weak leader.

# Chapter 10:
# All aboard the training bus

## Invest in your staff

### Common misconceptions

1. Good teachers were born to teach.

2. Professional development can be quantifiably measured, with an immediate impact on pupil learning.

3. Data is the key driver to measure the overall effectiveness of the quality of teaching.

A key consideration when considering how you invest in your staff is who can teach and what is good teaching? Some people take the view that good teachers were born to teach. That they were given a gift by the gods. Other people take the view that you can learn to teach with thousands of hours of practice and investment, whereas some people take the view that if you give people a list of core techniques then bingo. There are those who argue that teaching is a precise science. It is like medicine and we should engage all staff in hard quantitative evidence and research. Some people have seen it as wholly data driven and that the data is the determinant for how teacher X should engage in their craft.

Personally I would argue that teaching is a profession and should rightly remain so. In becoming a teacher you need to possess and develop specialist knowledge, expertise and a strong professional vocabulary. There are shared standards of practice within the profession and a long and rigorous process of training and qualifications are essential and required to become a teacher. There is also a commitment, albeit potentially unwritten, to continuous learning and professional upskilling. Our human and social capital is also critical to our ability to teach, as is our ability to make key decisions in split seconds and to reflect deeply about our own practice.

Wherever you reside on the spectrum of what makes a teacher and good teaching, you are dead in the water if you do not invest in your staff. Of anything within a school you must, must, must invest in your staff. It staggers me that CPD budgets are often given the least consideration. The staff working in our schools are invaluable. There is a real need to invest in their professional capital. This is also – I would like to add – a long-term process and not one that can have an instant and demonstrably measurable impact. Of course, teachers need to be highly committed to their craft but they also need to be properly prepared, trained and invested in. Any one given teacher can teach really well but they can only do so if they are shown what to do, have the right level of subject knowledge and are able to operate within a wider and highly professional subject community.

A huge issue for our profession is – and has been – the obsession with data, technology and narrow-driven tests. All of these factors, coupled with a bias towards entertaining, have served to systematically undermine the teacher as the expert. Some key questions that we need to consider when weighing up what we want from our teachers include:

- Is teaching technically difficult or technically quite simple but tiring?

- Do we value long periods of training or does teaching require a more limited intellectual ability?

- Does good teaching come over time, with continuous incremental improvements, or is it something that through hard work and determination can be mastered quite quickly?

- Are we better placed allowing teachers to use sound professional judgement that is informed by evidence and experience or is it better to drive staff with hard performance targets?

- Does good teaching come from a collective approach or is it purely down to working as an island?

- Is in-depth subject knowledge key or should teachers be trained in an array of pedagogical approaches that help facilitate learning?

My feelings steer towards the former rather than the latter of those questions. They are important questions to ask when considering what you want from your staffing body and how you will seek to support them in achieving it. I would also argue that a flawed view is that teaching should hurt. Why should it? Likewise, there has been a well held view that good teaching results in good behaviour. Again, I would really challenge this stance.

Earlier on in this book I cited that in order to lead you need to know yourself first. This is so true of how a senior leader drives staff professional development. You need to know within yourself, honestly and truthfully, what allowed you to teach successfully, what was tosh, what simply did not work, what made your life easier and what would have made your life easier. You also need to carefully consider what your frustrations were as a full time class teacher, how messages were conveyed to you and how you conveyed them to others. These are all important considerations when you consider how you will train your own staff, what you will train them in and how much you will, or will not, invest in them.

There is also a need to develop the wider human and social capital of your staffing body as a whole. There is a need to consider very carefully that the collective, and not the individual, are what makes a school strong. Pupils do well because they have a series of good teachers. This does not happen by chance but by design, investing and training.

With the collective in mind there is a need to give staff the time to work in teams, ideally as part of subject communities. Staff learn more and improve at a much faster rate if they are able to work, plan and be part of a wider team. Co-planning, training one another and sharing subject expertise are just a few of the benefits of being part of a subject-based community. The key, as with everything, is that you invest directed time to allow staff to work together to make this happen. Subject areas need time to work as a team. This will also improve communication and, invariably, reduce the need for emails. Institutionally such an approach will benefit the institutional culture. Of course, the key to the success of any given subject community is the middle leader who is in charge. Which is where training your middle leadership layer is critical.

We need to inspire teachers to invest in their own teaching. When I say invest, I mean see the worth in doing so and take the time, which schools should provide, to do so. A critical consideration is the opportunity cost of allowing staff the time, support and space to invest in developing their own teaching in a safe and risk-free manner.

I do subscribe to a view that research and quantitative evidence is key to improving and developing our profession. However, I also view research with a critical lens. Over the years research has championed many falsehoods. I would, therefore, encourage the profession to critically consider the self-interest and internal bias of the researcher. Also, whether the research is politically biased and whether it is approaching a matter from a very selective stance. We also need to carefully consider what the unintended consequences of a proposed approach may be and if we are going to promote something what else is going to give. We should also remember carefully that evidence can come from experience just as much as it can come from research.

I do think it is fair that as a profession we constantly develop and build our knowledge base; that we consider carefully where approaches fit a sitting and context best. I do promote the idea that teachers should be free to test out theories in their own class setting free from fear.

Equally as important is how newly qualified and new teachers to a school are supported. There needs to be a culture in all of our schools where new members of staff and new teachers are given bespoke training and support, that is targeted to their individual needs. These very colleagues should also be assigned a coach and mentor to help support them to transition into life at your school.

The approachability of the principal is also really important. Holding staff consultative forums on a termly basis can be an extremely supportive tool, where staff can present worries and concerns. Equally, and wherever possible, I have found that consultative forums on behaviour, the curriculum, teaching and learning and staff welfare have also been really useful. I would also advocate a principal meeting with NQTs on a half termly basis to discuss how they are being supported, settling in and if there is anything they need to support them. Furthermore, I think it is invaluable that a principal takes the time once a year to meet with every single member of staff for a one-to-one meeting. The focus of this meeting is purely to discuss them, their professional development, future plans and needs. Then, importantly, action any promises made.

I also go back to a point I made at the start of this chapter, teachers are professionals. With that in mind, do we need endless red tape? For example, colleague X needs to take the morning off for an urgent medical appointment. Do they really need to fill in three different forms to request this when a simple conversation would suffice? This is also a need for principals to be flexible with their staff. If colleague X requests time-off for something legitimate and pressing then careful consideration needs to be given to why the answer would be no.

We also need to consider how we support staff too. How much time do we give to faculty CPD, whole-school CPD, bringing in external CPD and external support. To what extent do we nurture and develop staff specialist knowledge, specifically subject knowledge? Professional development should be integral to a school improvement approach and sit at the heart of all staff considerations. We do want to develop, I would argue, a culture of restless and continuous improvement, with class practitioners striving to develop and evolve.

In my experience an ever-improving culture is generated through addressing workload and ensuring that whilst there is some accountability it becomes low stakes. There needs to be a strong emphasis on modelling and sharing good practice. Where quality assurance comes into play all feedback should be developmental and not judgemental. Grading staff on the alleged quality of their teaching and learning, the latter being impossible to measure, is reductive. Staff are far better to seek support for an area of their enacted pedagogical approach that they would like to develop over the course of a year and gain support and feedback in developing this. Why would telling a teacher they are a grade 3 ever be productive or helpful? With that in mind, any given member of staff should have their own personalised CPD pathway/menu that is bespoke to them and their personal professional needs.

Departmental/subject communities are a fantastic vehicle for supporting the development of subject knowledge. Through communities like this you can develop a common set of threshold concepts and powerful knowledge that underpins your curriculum area. You can then train one another where people have gaps and areas of expertise. Subject teams can also construct reading lists for staff professional development and then discuss these texts. The same for blogs and key journals. This allows members of a team to capitalise of the expertise of their colleagues, discussing tricky aspects of the curriculum. Such communities also allow groups of teachers to map out curricular designs, explore curriculum intent and implementation and discuss in depth where the curriculum has and has not worked.

## Final thoughts

As the final chapter of this book draws to a close, some key points to consider include:

1. Teaching is a highly-skilled profession, requiring high levels of specialist-subject knowledge.

2. Professional development requires huge investment, both in terms of time and money.

3. Those delivering training to staff must never forget what it is like to be a front line teacher, teaching four or five lessons a day, every day.

4. We need to inspire teachers to invest in their own learning and provide them with the time, space, freedom and opportunities to do so.

# Final musings

# Concluding thoughts

Within this book I have detailed a number of core areas that help to support a school in moving forwards. In Chapter 1 I discussed the importance of leadership, of understanding yourself and the type of leader that you are. In Chapter 2 I considered how you prepare yourself in anticipation of making that step up and the overall vision and strategy to employ. In Chapter 3 we considered the importance of behaviour, routines for learning and institutional procedures. Chapter 4 built on this by considering what we permit we promote and the role of exclusions.

Chapters 5 and 6 honed in on the importance and role of knowledge and the curriculum as a progression model. This was then reinforced by chapters seven and eight, which championed the teacher ultimately as the expert in the classroom. Chapter 9 considered how we can support staff in reducing workload and Chapter 10 was a call to arms, detailing the need to invest richly in staff and their professional development.

As I draw this book to a close I would argue that school improvement comes from the clever interplay and inter-relationship of the following factors working in unison:

The inter-connected relationship of all of the above factors and how they work together, almost embryonically, is key to a school's success.

If I were Ofsted, which has deliberately not been mentioned throughout this book, then I would focus on some of the following questions to address if a school is indeed improving and driving positive change:

- How do you self-evaluate?

- What is your approach to professional development and what is the impact of that approach?

- How do you undertake school improvement?

- What is the purpose of your curriculum? What do you expect and hope pupils to learn, know and understand by the end of Year 7, 9, 11 or 13?

- What is your school's culture?

- What is behaviour like in your school on a typical day?

- What has been done to support succession planning?

- What support and training do staff receive?

- How do you academically challenge your pupils?

- How do you enrich your curriculum?

- What do you teach in subject X? When? Why?

- How do you support pupils with additional needs?

So, to conclude this book I feel we should never lose sight of the following, which are key to all schools:

- **A clear drive from the top:** As a principal, if you allow it, over 80% of your role can focus on irrelevant paperwork, emails and whistling to the tune of other people. Your high level and consistent visibility is incredibly important. It is easy, however, to be artificially visible. Active visibility, where you involve yourself directly in the school and its actual running is key

- **Back to basics:** Consider carefully how you want your school to look, to feel, what the culture, climate and ethos should be like.

- **An open approach:** Be really clear with what you want. Ensure this is clearly conveyed to everyone; governors, trustees, SLT, parents, staff and students.

- **Staff buy-in:** For me this is the big one. Are the staff behind your vision and your approach? Have you invested in them to believe in you, what you are doing and how? Have you trained all your staff to think and act in a way that you want them to?

- **Consistency:** I do not believe or buy into the view that if you teach well then the students will behave. Without boundaries and a consistent school-wide approach nothing works. Believing that great teaching leads to great behaviour is a myth. Children love and thrive off structure, boundaries and consistency.

- **Directive teaching:** The teacher should be hailed as the expert. Teacher subject knowledge is key and the content, not the activities, is the engager.

- **The curriculum is God:** The curriculum is key. Think carefully about how the curriculum operates as a story for any one given subject domain. What is it that you want the pupils to know at the end of that story?

It is important to remember that lasting change does not come overnight. Quick wins can be made in schools and band aids can often be used to paper over the cracks in a school. However, slow change is lasting change and lasting change brings about true success. Ultimately, you permit what you promote and you promote what you permit.

Thank you for reading this book and I hope, at the very least, it helps you to consider how to drive and improve your own school.